# Landmarks of BRITAIN

## LISA PRITCHARD

MYRIAD
LONDON

# CONTENTS

Title page: Stonehenge;
opposite: Rannoch Moor

First published in 2006 by
Myriad Books Limited
35 Bishopsthorpe Road, London
SE26 4PA

ISBN 1 904 736 25 4

Designed by Jerry Goldie Graphic Design

Printed in China

www.myriadbooks.com

# INTRODUCTION

First-time visitors to the UK are often surprised to find that in a day's drive you pass through such a variety of scenery. Less than two hours south of London, the iconic white cliffs drop away to the English Channel. To the south-west, the Devon and Cornwall peninsula offers the wide-open spaces of Exmoor, Dartmoor and Bodmin Moor that contrast with ever-narrower lanes and a stunning coastline.

Head west from the capital and you can enjoy the gentle rolling Cotswold Hills before reaching Wales and discovering the beauty of the Gower Peninsula and Snowdonia.

To the east lie the flatlands of Cambridgeshire and the Norfolk Broads, where the horizon seems endless and you can glide along the waterways in a boat, watching the rich birdlife or simply enjoying the peace and quiet.

Strike out northwards and the choice is yours: the breathtaking scenery of the Lake District, the riches of Yorkshire's dales and moors, or the grandeur of the Pennines and the Peak District. Cross the border into Scotland and the landscape unfolds with a seemingly infinite variety of wooded hills, heather-covered moors and lochs.

The rich history of Britain's inhabitants is an integral part of the country you see today. You can visit the stupendous giant stones of Stonehenge, raised some 4,000 years ago, walk through fields with drystone walls, see brick-and-flint houses, thatched cottages, imposing castles and elegant stately homes. Tradition is strong in historic cities such as Oxford. Meanwhile the 21st century is firmly embraced in major centres such as Manchester, London, Cardiff and Glasgow where old treasures are complemented by bold high-tech architecture.

These pages reflect some of the most visited and best-loved gems of England, Scotland and Wales – the landmarks of Britain.

*Lisa Pritchard*

# WESTMINSTER

## *London SW1*

For the British, the single word "Westminster" encompasses the parliamentary establishment. From Westminster Bridge (above right) you can see the Palace of Westminster, home of both the House of Commons and the House of Lords. The eastern end of the palace is dominated by the Clock Tower with its great bell, Big Ben. The combined length of the "corridors of power" and rather less important passages in the maze-like palace is more than 2 miles (3km).

A stone's throw away stands Westminster Abbey (above), the focal point for many national events from coronations to royal weddings and state funerals. Indeed, this is a place of pilgrimage for many as some of the nation's key poets, musicians, writers and politicians are buried here. Memorials include the tomb of Queen Elizabeth I (below right) and a statue of Shakespeare in Poets' Corner (far right).

Outside in Parliament Square stands a statue of Sir Winston Churchill (above), Britain's wartime prime minister and a towering influence in the first half of the 20th century – a man many still consider to be Britain's greatest politician. It is a short walk across the square and down Whitehall to Downing Street.

## Worth a visit

# TRAFALGAR SQUARE

## *London SW1*

The northern side of Trafalgar Square is dominated by the National Gallery, home to one of the world's premier collections of European paintings, with masterpieces such as the *Madonna of the Pinks*. Curiously, this is also where the UK's imperial measurements of length (inches, feet and yards) are literally set in stone, under the balustrade.

Every year Nelson's Column has to compete with an enormous Christmas tree (above) in Trafalgar Square, a gift from the people of Norway to thank the British for helping to liberate them at the end of the Second World War. It's an uplifting sight throughout December, the beautiful tree and the illuminated fountains playing.

Come January Nelson's Column (left) and his four bronze lions return to centre stage. Massive classical sculptures are mounted on three of the four plinths on the square. The fourth plinth currently showcases modern sculptures for six months at a time.

# BUCKINGHAM PALACE

*London SW1*

Amust-see on every tourist's itinerary today, Buckingham Palace has not always been the symbol of the royal household. When George III bought the Duke of Buckingham's townhouse in 1761, it was simply one of the Royal Family's many private houses. His flamboyant son George IV (1820-30) commissioned John Nash to redesign the building but died before it was finished. His brother William IV, rather unenthusiastic about the project, offered Buckingham Palace to Parliament after fire destroyed the Palace of Westminster in 1835. But Parliament refused and rebuilt Westminster instead.

Two years later Queen Victoria made Buckingham Palace her official residence. It was very grand but impractical with poor ventilation and smoking chimneys. Her husband Prince Albert reorganised the household and resolved the problems.

Today the palace still doubles as the head office for the monarchy and the Queen's home. It has 19 staterooms, 52 principal bedrooms and 188 bedrooms for staff, and 92 offices. The Queen's private rooms are in the north wing of the palace.

In mid-June each year the Queen (far right, leaving Buckingham Palace in an open-topped carriage) marks her official birthday at the Trooping of the Colour ceremony in nearby Horseguards' Parade.

## Worth a visit

# TOWER OF LONDON AND TOWER BRIDGE

*Tower Hill, London EC3*

WORTH A VISIT

CITY HALL

HMS BELFAST

ST KATHARINE DOCKS

HAY'S GALLERIA

DOCKLANDS LIGHT RAILWAY

London's ancient fortress, the Tower of London, is one of the capital's key tourist attractions, renowned for the Crown Jewels, the Yeomen Warders (Beefeaters) and its imposing stone towers. The White Tower was built by the Normans. In the Middle Ages the Tower of London was a royal residence, but in Tudor times it became a notorious prison. Those who fell from grace, such as Henry VIII's wives Anne Boleyn and Catherine Howard, arrived by river at the Traitor's Gate. Few survived – most were incarcerated in one of the towers and later beheaded. The walls of the Beauchamp Tower still bear inscriptions (right) etched by desperate prisoners all too aware of their destiny.

Tower Bridge (above) was opened in 1894 to service the expanding business area in the East End of London. Its central span splits into two sections that are raised to allow tall vessels to pass through to the port facilities upriver in the Port of London. Visitors can view London from the raised walkway.

# St Paul's Cathedral

*Ludgate Hill, London EC4*

Sir Christopher Wren oversaw the rebuilding of more than 50 churches in the City of London, lost in the Great Fire of 1666. His first design for the new cathedral was based on a Greek cross, with four equal arms, but Church Commissioners insisted on the traditional Latin cross, with a long nave and short transepts. Wren's dome remains a hallmark of the cathedral, and is often used in movies as a single image to place the action in London.

Thirty-five years after building work began, the 79-year-old architect saw his vision completed. You can walk up the 259 steps to the Whispering Gallery inside the dome: if you whisper to the wall, someone standing on the opposite side will hear you clearly. The Stone and Golden Galleries offer panoramic views of London.

The composer Felix Mendelssohn once played the organ here. It is housed in an intricate case by master woodcarver Grinling Gibbons, and has 7,189 pipes and 138 stops.

## WORTH A VISIT

MILLENNIUM BRIDGE

TATE MODERN

ST BRIDE'S CHURCH, FLEET STREET

MUSEUM OF LONDON

THE MONUMENT

BANK OF ENGLAND, THE ROYAL EXCHANGE AND MANSION HOUSE

# LONDON EYE

## *South Bank, London SE1*

The delicate circle of the London Eye seems virtually transparent when you see it from far away. Very popular, it is London's fourth tallest structure and the largest observation wheel in the world; it takes half an hour to turn a full revolution.

Just across the Thames from the Houses of Parliament, the Eye opened in March 2000. Its original five-year licence has been extended for a further 24 years. The Eye is suspended over the river, with A-frame legs grounded on the south bank. The parts were so large they had to be manufactured in sections and assembled on the spot before being hoisted into position.

Step aboard one of the 32 "pods" on a clear day and for the next 30 minutes you will be sure of some of the best views of London. When the weather is at its best you can see for 25 miles (40km) in each direction. The Eye is in constant motion, revolving at about 0.6mph (0.9km an hour).

# GLOBE THEATRE

## *Bankside, London SE1*

This faithful replica of the O-shaped Elizabethan playhouse owes its existence to the American actor-director Sam Wanamaker. He was astounded that Britain could allow the original Globe theatre, where William Shakespeare made his name 400 years ago, to vanish without trace just as the Puritans intended when they pulled it down in 1644.

Wanamaker's campaign culminated in the new Globe just 200 metres away from the original site, complete with thatched roof, lime plaster walls, wooden galleries and open-air auditorium.

When it opened in 1997, the public and theatre critics alike greeted it with great scepticism but it has since become one of the most successful theatres in Europe. Incredibly, it runs at a profit with no government subsidy, despite offering cheap tickets for the "groundlings", who stand in the pit.

The theatre's season runs from May to early October, but you can visit the theatre and the UnderGlobe, its exhibition space, all year round for an insight into Shakespeare's London in the early 17th century.

## Worth a visit

Southwark Cathedral

Jubilee Walkway

Design Museum

Borough Market

# ROYAL ALBERT HALL

*Kensington Gore, London SW3*

O f London's many concert venues and theatres, the Royal Albert Hall (far right and below) is surely the best known worldwide. It is the home of the annual summer season of BBC Proms concerts, as well as countless other performances.

This is yet another grand building with education and enlightenment at its heart that resulted from the Great Exhibition of 1851. The sum of £200,000 was spent to erect it "for the Advancement of the Arts and Sciences, and works of industry of all nations, in fulfilment of the intentions of Albert, Prince Consort". Its bold iron and glass dome rises to 835ft (275m) and it seats over 5,200 people.

Prince Albert died before the hall was completed. On the other side of Kensington Gore stands the Albert Memorial (right), raised by Victoria in memory of her beloved husband.

### WORTH A VISIT

KENSINGTON PALACE AND THE COURT DRESS COLLECTION

HYDE PARK AND THE SERPENTINE GALLERY

PICCADILLY

KENSINGTON MUSEUMS

# KENSINGTON MUSEUMS

*London SW7*

The cluster of museums along Cromwell Road in Kensington largely owe their existence to Prince Albert's grand scheme, the Great Exhibition of 1851.

The Victoria and Albert Museum (left), better known as the V&A, is renowned for its collections of paintings and sculpture, especially early Italian works. Here you will find Canova's *Three Graces*, and Raphael's cartoons for the tapestries in the Sistine Chapel. The wide-ranging collections of some four million items include glass, textiles, ceramics and jewellery.

Step through the imposing entrance of the nearby Natural History Museum (right) and you are immediately faced with a huge *Diplodocus* skeleton in the Central Hall, a stunning introduction to the museum's collection of fossilised dinosaur skeletons and a favourite with younger visitors. The museum's 70 million items take a long view of Earth's animal, plant and mineral riches.

Tucked behind is the Science Museum (far right). Another very popular destination for children, it vividly shows the impact of science in shaping modern life and offers fantastic hands-on workshops and demonstrations that may literally make your hair stand on end.

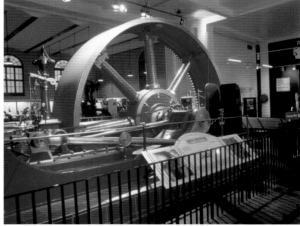

## WORTH A VISIT

BROMPTON ORATORY

HARRODS

KENSINGTON GARDENS AND HYDE PARK

ROYAL ALBERT HALL

ALBERT MEMORIAL

# TATE BRITAIN AND TATE MODERN

## *Millbank, London SW1 and Bankside, London SE1*

A significant part of Britain's art heritage is based on the humble sugar lump. Henry Tate started as a grocer's apprentice in Lancashire, and eventually made his fortune by refining sugar. He gave his huge collection of Victorian art to the nation, and paid for the first Tate Gallery at Millbank. The Tate went on to build a definitive collection of contemporary art throughout the next century, expanding to include foreign and Modernist works.

Regional galleries in Liverpool (1988) and St Ives (1993) were followed by the addition of a bold new

installation at London's old Bankside power station, now renamed Tate Modern. The collection is now divided into British and Modern art – the original gallery, renamed Tate Britain, shows British art from 1500 to the present, while Tate Modern houses Modern art from 1900 on.

Tate Britain runs the Turner Prize, an annual competition for artists under 50. This is a frequent source of controversy: each year critics loudly question whether the entries qualify as art.

### WORTH A VISIT

GLOBE THEATRE

MILLENNIUM BRIDGE

JUBILEE WALKWAY

FASHION AND TEXTILE MUSEUM

VINOPOLIS

## WORTH A VISIT

# GREENWICH

*Greenwich Royal Park, London SE10*

The home of Greenwich Mean Time and the Prime Meridian line (0 degrees longitude), Greenwich has played a pivotal role in the history of science. The Royal Observatory (above) was designed by Sir Christopher Wren in 1675. Here you can stand with one foot in the eastern and the other in the western hemisphere.

Nineteen years later, the Old Royal Naval College (left) was built "for the relief and support of seamen and their dependents and for the improvement of navigation". Other famous architects such as Vanbrugh and Hawksmoor later enhanced Wren's original design. From 1873 to 1998 the elegant building housed the Royal Naval College, and today it is shared by the University of Greenwich and Trinity College of Music.

The tea clipper *Cutty Sark* sits in dry dock by the river at the heart of Greenwich. Now a museum ship, it was launched in 1869 to compete in bringing the first tea of the year from China to England and later used to ship wool from Australia. In the 1920s it became a stationary training ship.

# KEW GARDENS

*Kew, Richmond*

Kew remains a world leader in plant conservation and research 250 years since it was founded. By the end of the 18th century, the keeper Sir Joseph Banks had already established plants from the six continents.

The gardens offer spectacular species to see all through the year. Equally dramatic are the 19th and 20th century glasshouses built to provide perfect microclimates to enable tropical and subtropical plants to thrive. Decimus Burton designed the huge Temperate House (above), the largest Victorian glass structure still standing. It covers 52,528sq ft (4,880sq m) and still follows his geographical scheme of planting for tender woody plants.

In 1987 the Princess of Wales

Conservatory (below, far left) was opened in memory of George III's mother Augusta, who first established the gardens. Much of the space is underground, with 10 computer-controlled environments, to cater for plants from extreme desert conditions to dense, humid rainforests.

The 10-storey, octagonal Pagoda (left) is a folly dating from the earliest days of the gardens, when Chinoiserie was all the rage. The rather more solid Dutch-influenced Kew Palace (below) was the home of George III, his wife Queen Charlotte and their large family.

### WORTH A VISIT

KEW GARDENS' MANY GLASSHOUSES, INCLUDING THE PALM HOUSE, TEMPERATE HOUSE AND PRINCESS OF WALES CONSERVATORY

WAKEHURST PLACE, SUSSEX

RHS GARDEN, WISLEY, SURREY

# HAMPTON COURT

## *East Molesley, Surrey*

When Cardinal Thomas Wolsey, Henry VIII's Lord Chancellor, failed to persuade the Pope to annul Henry's marriage to Catherine of Aragon, he fell from favour. In a desperate and ultimately unsuccessful attempt to regain his position in 1525, Wolsey gave Henry all his land and houses including Hampton Court. This became Henry's favourite palace, and he added the Great Hall as well as the Real Tennis courts. In 1689 Sir Christopher Wren remodelled the King's and Queen's apartments. Queen Victoria opened Hampton Court to the public in 1838.

The most famous part of the gardens is the hedge maze, with more than half a mile of paths, that was planted in the late 17th century. Elsewhere avenues laid out by William III radiate from the house, through 60 acres of formal parterres and "wilderness" gardens along the river Thames (left).

Visitors today can see the Tudor kitchens (right) and the state apartments, and stroll in the courtyards and gardens. The annual Hampton Court Flower Show in July attracts thousands of enthusiastic gardeners.

WORTH A VISIT

HOME PARK

BUSHY PARK

GARRICK'S TEMPLE TO SHAKESPEARE

TEDDINGTON LOCK

# WINDSOR AND ETON

*Berkshire*

When the Queen is at Windsor Castle, the Royal Standard flies from the Round Tower. The castle has been inhabited for 900 years, perched on a hill in the centre of Windsor, a bustling town on the banks of the Thames (right).

St George's Chapel (above, left of picture) within the castle grounds, dates from 1475. It is the home of the Order of the Garter, the highest order of chivalry the Queen can bestow. Henry VIII and Charles I are among the monarchs buried in the chapel, as are the Queen Mother and the Queen's younger sister, Princess Margaret, who died in 2002.

Down in the town, Burford House (far right) on Church Street belonged to Nell Gwynn – ideally placed close to the castle gardens for her liaison with Charles II.

Cross Windsor Bridge and you come to Eton, home of the largest independent school in Britain. Parents pay more than £20,000 a year for their son's education at Eton College (right) – a far cry from Henry IV's intent in 1440 when he founded Eton as a charity school.

Left: schoolboys at Eton. Famous Old Etonians include 18 former British prime ministers and 24 members of royal families

AD 1640

IN THIS HISTORIC HOUSE Nell Gwynn LIVED

## Worth a Visit

Windsor Great Park

Savill Gardens

Runnymede

Ascot races

Henley-on-Thames: hire a boat on the Thames

# CANTERBURY

*Kent*

Canterbury was already an important city in the Middle Ages: the seat of the Archbishop of Canterbury and a staging post between London and the south coast. The Norman cathedral still towers over the city today.

Henry II's bitter dispute with his Archbishop of Canterbury, Thomas Becket, lasted eight years. Becket refused to acknowledge the state's supremacy over the church. In 1170 Henry's men murdered the Archbishop in the cathedral. Pilgrims flocked to his tomb, inspiring Chaucer's *Canterbury Tales*. Beside Becket is the tomb of Edward III's son, the Black Prince (below right) a key figure in England's battles with France in the 14th century.

Canterbury Cathedral, its precinct, St Augustine's Abbey and St Martin's Church have been designated a World Heritage Site. The modern city is compact and cosmopolitan. The river Stour flows through it, and half-timbered houses such as the medieval Weavers' Houses (above left) still stand. The weavers were Huguenots who fled from France to escape persecution – today the restored houses are restaurants and shops.

# WHITE CLIFFS OF DOVER

### *Kent*

For sheer drama in terms of landscape it is hard to beat the White Cliffs of Dover. They tower over the port with the town tucked into the narrow strip of land at their feet (below). The cliffs form part of the North Downs, and are visible for miles.

The Roman lighthouse still stands on the clifftop, as does Dover Castle (far right and below). From the Normans to the 20th century, this remained strategically important. Miles of tunnels inside the soft chalk and black flint of the cliff provided barracks during the Napoleonic Wars, and were used as an underground military command centre and hospital during the evacuation of Dunkirk in the Second World War.

Dover is just 21 miles (34km) from Calais, the shortest distance between France and England. It has survived the opening of the Channel Tunnel and the cross-channel port (right) remains one of the UK's busiest with 18 million ferry passengers every year.

## WORTH A VISIT

SOUTH FORELAND
CASTLE

TIMEBALL TOWER,
DEAL

DEAL CASTLE

WALMER CASTLE

NORTH DOWNS
WAY

BATTLE OF BRITAIN
MUSEUM,
HAWKINGE

# BEACHY HEAD

### *Near Eastbourne, Sussex*

## WORTH A VISIT

SOUTH DOWNS WAY

MICHELHAM PRIORY, UPPER DICKER

ALFRISTON CLERGY HOUSE

BATTLE

GREAT DIXTER

On a clear day there are truly stunning views from the top of Britain's highest chalk sea cliff, Beachy Head (right, 580ft/162m). Eastwards lies Eastbourne and Hastings. To the west you can see Newhaven and Brighton, and sometimes you can even glimpse the Isle of Wight.

The lighthouse was originally built 540ft (165m) out from the base of the cliffs, but in 1999 a huge chunk of the cliffs slipped down into the sea, and now the land almost reaches to the foot of the lighthouse.

Stretching away from Beachy Head, the rounded Seven Sisters cliffs (top) have been a crucial landmark for sailors for centuries. At the western end is Cuckmere Haven, where the South Downs meet the sea. It is in turn sheltered by Seaford Head, home to an important nature reserve. About 1ft (30cm) of cliff is lost to erosion every year.

# SOUTH DOWNS

*From East Sussex to Hampshire*

WORTH A VISIT

LONG MAN OF WILMINGTON

MONK'S HOUSE, RODMELL

DEVIL'S DYKE

PARHAM HOUSE, STORRINGTON

DUNCTON HILL

UPPARK, SOUTH HARTING

The South Downs run about 70 miles (100 km) across the south of England from Eastbourne in Sussex to Winchester in Hampshire. A popular trail, the South Downs Way, follows this ridge of chalk downland, much of which is an area of outstanding natural beauty.

Six miles north-west of Eastbourne stands the Long Man of Wilmington (above) on Windover Hill. The first known drawing of this 227ft (69m) figure dates back to 1710, but nobody really knows when it was first etched into the hillside.

The view from Ditchling Beacon (far right), 3.5 miles (6km) north of Brighton, is rightly famous. This is the highest point in Sussex, and was one of a chain of beacons where bonfires were lit to signal an attack.

Opera buffs flock to the annual summer season at Glyndebourne (right) as they have since 1934. Tradition demands a champagne picnic in the grounds during the interval.

# THE SOLENT

*The channel between Portsmouth and the Isle of Wight*

The Solent separates the Isle of Wight from the British mainland. It is a busy waterway: as well as ferries bustling across to the Isle of Wight and the occasional passing of Royal Navy vessels, it teems with yachts of all kinds especially during Cowes Week in August every year.

The sheltered waters of the Solent made Portsmouth an ideal port for a seafaring nation. Families still gather on the Round Tower (above) to wave goodbye to sailors on board Royal Navy ships as they sail out from the harbour. In 1545 Henry VIII watched his great flagship the *Mary Rose* sink here as she sailed into battle against the French.

A somewhat happier destiny brought *HMS Victory* in to dry dock in Portsmouth. Admiral Nelson's flagship is the world's oldest commissioned warship. It is both the flagship of the current Second Sea Lord and a living museum to the Georgian navy.

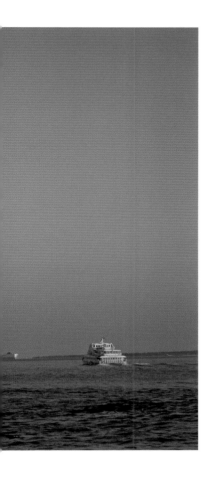

# ISLE OF WIGHT

*Five miles south of Portsmouth*

The Isle of Wight is often considered to be a reflection of what England used to be. It sits, diamond-shaped, just 30 minutes by ferry across the Solent from Portsmouth. The red squirrel, almost wiped out on the mainland, still thrives on the island.

At its western end, the Needles, a series of chalk stacks, march out to sea. They are quite stubby – the formation was named after a needle-shaped column that stood in the middle until storms caused its collapse in 1764. On the outermost rock sits the unmanned Needles Lighthouse (right).

When Queen Victoria and Prince Albert began to spend their summers at Osborne House near Cowes (below) the island became very fashionable. Today's tourists may be a little surprised to learn that the royal couple considered this magnificent house with its gilt and marble "a modest country home". Cowes' August sailing regatta and the Isle of Wight music festival attract thousands of visitors every year.

WORTH A
VISIT

ISLE OF WIGHT
STEAM RAILWAY

BRADING ROMAN
VILLA

ALUM BAY

THE NEEDLES
OLD BATTERY

HAMSTEAD
HERITAGE COAST

# WINCHESTER

## *Hampshire*

WORTH A VISIT

FARLEY MOUNT

MOTTISFONT ABBEY

NORTHINGTON GRANGE

AVINGTON PARK

HINTON AMPNER

Winchester, where modern cricket began and the novelist Jane Austen is buried, was once the capital of King Alfred the Great's kingdom of Wessex. With the rise of London, Winchester remained an important centre for learning and religious affairs.

To stand in the Cathedral Close when Winchester Cathedral's 14 bells are rung is simply breathtaking. Thirty-five English kings were crowned here, and 20 of them buried, including King Canute. St Swithin was Bishop of Winchester in the 9th century: legend has it that rain on St Swithin's Day (July 15) means rain for the next 40 days.

When Oliver Cromwell demolished Winchester Castle he kept the vaulted Great Hall (above) for assemblies and County Assizes. In pride of place hangs a huge 14th-century table, rumoured for centuries to have been the Round Table of the legendary King Arthur and his famous knights.

Today the county town of Hampshire prides itself on good food and a lively arts and crafts scene.

# SALISBURY

*South Wiltshire*

The soaring beauty of Salisbury Cathedral (above) remains a wonder of 13th-century craftsmanship. The spire, completed a generation later in 1333, is the tallest in Britain today. Inside you will find the oldest working clock in Europe, dating from 1386, as well as one of the four surviving original versions of the Magna Carta, signed by King John at Runnymede in 1215.

On a summer's day, the lush acres of the huge Cathedral Close (left) offer quintessentially English sights such as cricket matches. A gate to the close (above) leads you into Salisbury's busy high street where the medieval mixes happily with the modern.

Salisbury is sometimes referred to as New Sarum. Just to the north of the present Salisbury is Old Sarum, an Iron Age hillfort where you can still find traces of the old Norman cathedral and castle. When the medieval city outgrew Old Sarum, the present cathedral was founded and the whole settlement followed.

## WORTH A VISIT

STONEHENGE

OLD SARUM

HEALE GARDENS

FIGSBURY RING

WILTON HOUSE

BREAMORE HOUSE

# STONEHENGE

*Salisbury Plain, Wiltshire*

Every year about 20,000 people mark the summer solstice at Stonehenge on Salisbury Plain. Its origins are still shrouded in mystery. Was it a giant astronomical observatory, or a sacred burial site? And how did primitive people transport these huge stones and set them into the ground so that they are still in position 4,000 years later?

This megalithic stone circle was clearly an astounding feat of engineering. The smaller bluestones in the inner circle, weighing about four tonnes each, are thought to have come from south-west Wales. The giant sarsen stones (above) probably came from the Marlborough Downs, 20 miles away. They weigh anything up to 50 tonnes, and historians reckon at least 600 men would have been needed to bring each stone up the steepest part of the route.

The alignment of these iconic stones is very precisely north/east and south/west. When the sun rises on equinox and solstice mornings its rays stream through the gaps in the stones. Stonehenge still inspires awe even in the most cynical observer today.

## WORTH A VISIT

SALISBURY

WOODHENGE

AVEBURY CIRCLE

WESTBURY WHITE HORSE,
ONE OF FIVE IN THE AREA

SILBURY HILL

# DARTMOOR

*Devon*

The bleak splendour of Dartmoor's granite outcrops and boggy moorland stretches across a great swathe of the West Country, bounded by Okehampton, Ivybridge, Tavistock and Bovey Tracey. Walkers may see occasional groups of Dartmoor ponies running free, as well as skylarks, ring ouzels and birds of prey.

Dartmoor has more than 160 high rocky hills known as tors. A perfect example is Combestone Tor (above) which overlooks the valley of the river Dart. Perhaps the most popular of all is Hay Tor (far right) in east Dartmoor. Its fine granite was mined throughout the 19th century for buildings such as the British Museum and the old London Bridge. Every year 2,500 young people take part in the gruelling two-day Ten Tors race.

You will also find some picture-book villages, such as Buckland in the Moor (right). Its 15th-century church has a remarkable clockface – it has no numbers, but letters that spell out "My Dear Mother".

# LAND'S END

*Cornwall*

## WORTH A VISIT

MINACK OPEN AIR
THEATRE AND
GARDENS

MERRY MAIDENS
STONE CIRCLE

GEEVOR TIN MINE

SOUTH-WEST
COASTAL PATH

TRENGWAINTON
GARDEN

The westernmost tip of mainland Britain is on the Penwith peninsula, near Penzance in Cornwall. This is not the soft chalk of the White Cliffs of Dover, but granite.

While Land's End is a popular tourist destination, its name is most often heard in connection with sponsored fundraising attempts to walk, run or cycle the full length of Britain from Land's End in the extreme south-west to John O'Groats, the north-eastern tip of Scotland. The same company owns both sites, and has even designated an official start and finish line for "end to enders".

Not surprisingly, the company is happy to encourage visitors into its gift shop, café and exhibition, or to have their picture taken at the

signpost (above) showing the distance to Liverpool and New York. A windy walk along the clifftop soon restores your sense of wonder as you gaze out to the Longships Lighthouse (right) a few miles out to sea.

# BATH

*Somerset*

Other than London, Bath is perhaps the city that most completely reflects England's history. In one short walking tour you can visit the Roman Baths (far right) which were built at a spring venerated by the Celts, then wander on to Bath Abbey, and later the Royal Crescent.

The Abbey (right) began life as a monastic church in AD675 and was raised to a cathedral in 1090. However it was allowed to fall into disrepair, and was stripped bare by Henry VIII in 1539. A generation later it was restored as Bath's grand parish church. Under Elizabeth I Bath began to prosper once again, and the spa was revived.

Bath's popularity soared during the Georgian era when some of its most enduring architectural gems were built, such as the Royal Crescent (below) and other fine terraces of townhouses. The pale Bath stone used throughout the city has created a wonderfully harmonious whole.

Modern Bath trades on its beauty and history, and tourism remains its principal industry.

## WORTH A VISIT

ROMAN BATHS AND PUMP ROOM

BECKFORD'S TOWER

RADSTOCK MUSEUM

AVON VALLEY RAILWAY

WESTWOOD MANOR

GREAT CHALFIELD MANOR

# COTSWOLDS

*Oxfordshire, Gloucestershire and south Warwickshire*

The warm Cotswold stone is one of the attractions of the towns and villages in these hills. This area of central England prospered from the wool trade in the 15th and 16th centuries, when many cottages, manor houses and churches were built in the local honey-coloured limestone.

Lower Slaughter (above, right) sits either side of a stream, the Eye. Far from being an echo of past barbarity, the village's name simply means "wet land". Much of Stanton (below, centre) is relatively unchanged in 300 years. Set below Shenbarrow Hill, the old houses on its main street have typical steeply pitched gables and mullioned windows.

When the wool trade tailed off, the village of Blockley (above) began to produce silk. In the 19th century six mills were spinning silk thread for Coventry's

flourishing ribbon manufacturers.

Twenty miles west of Oxford, Burford is often called the gateway to the Cotswolds. In 1649 Oliver Cromwell imprisoned 340 dissenting Puritans known as the Levellers in its fine church, before shooting the three ringleaders. A detail from the churchyard is shown (right).

## WORTH A VISIT

WESTONBIRT ARBORETUM

CHAVENAGE, TETBURY

BOURTON-ON-THE-WATER

PRINKNASH ABBEY

PAINSWICK AND ROCOCO
GARDENS

# OXFORD

## *Oxfordshire*

Matthew Arnold's often-quoted description of Oxford as "that sweet city with her dreaming spires" still rings true today. The town is dominated by its ancient university, founded in the 12th century, and the colleges jostle close to one another in the centre. Each college is autonomous; many were built around a quadrangle in order to enhance the feeling of community.

As you walk under Hertford College's bridge (far right), known to many as the Bridge of Sighs, you may agree it is closer in design to Venice's Rialto Bridge. Completed in 1914, it is a relative youngster – many of the city's best-known buildings are much older. The Radcliffe Camera (right) was opened in 1749 to house a science library for the university. Today it is a history and English reading room for the Bodleian Library.

Christ Church (below right) is also the cathedral of Oxford. Magdalene College (below), with its famous bridge, is well-known for its May Day celebrations.

## WORTH A VISIT

CHRIST CHURCH CATHEDRAL

THE COLLEGES – TAKE A WALKING
TOUR

BOTANICAL GARDENS

CARFAX TOWER

ASHMOLEAN MUSEUM

UNIVERSITY PARKS AND
MESOPOTAMIA

PITT RIVERS MUSEUM

59

# BLENHEIM

*Woodstock, Oxfordshire*

Blenheim was named after one of the most important military victories of John Churchill, the first Duke of Marlborough, in 1704. Queen Anne was so grateful that she granted him Woodstock and declared she would build him a house at her own expense. In the event, the Duke had to pay more than £45,000 to finish the work.

The palace retains a strong flavour of that era. The tapestry on the wall of the Green Writing Room (above) shows the Duke accepting the French surrender at the Battle of Blenheim, while in the Long Library (far right, top) there are full-length paintings of Queen Anne, William III and the Duke. At the library's north end the highly decorated Willis organ dates from 1891.

Marlborough's most illustrious descendant was the statesman, prime minister and author Sir Winston Churchill (1874-1965). After a state funeral he was buried in the graveyard of Bladon Church on the Blenheim estate.

WORTH A
VISIT

WOODSTOCK

NORTH LEIGH
ROMAN VILLA

ROLLRIGHT
STONES

WADDESDON
MANOR

Top: the Long Library, Blenheim; above: Sir Winston Churchill's grave in the churchyard at Bladon

# CAMBRIDGE

*Cambridgeshire*

One in five of Cambridge's population is a student at the university. It dates back to the early 13th century, when students fled from violence in Oxford and set up in this small town on the banks of the river Cam. The town has grown up around the classically beautiful buildings of the 31 colleges and their grounds.

The façade of King's College Chapel (above right) is one of the most beautiful sights of Cambridge. Every year, the Christmas Eve service is broadcast live across the world.

Stand on King's Bridge and look towards Clare College (above) and you will see students and tourists punting along the river. A similar tradition exists in Oxford, although the punting technique is slightly different. The rivalry between Cambridge and Oxford reaches its peak in the annual University Boat Race on the Thames in London.

Trinity College (far right) is the university's richest college. Many illustrious students have passed through this gate, including 31 Nobel Laureates.

## Worth a visit

Anglesey Abbey

Wimpole Hall and
Home Farm

Wandlebury

Chilford Hundred
vineyard

Houghton Mill

Wicken Fen

# NORFOLK BROADS

*Norfolk*

The shallow lakes and rivers of the Broads are largely manmade, the result of more than 350 years' intensive digging of peat (turf) for fuel. The pits where the peat had been dug away gradually filled with water and by the 14th century the peat could no longer be reached. The land flooded, forming the wetlands known today as the Norfolk and Suffolk Broads.

You won't travel far along the waterways before you see a windmill – and then another, and another, built to aid drainage. Many picturesque windmills such as Hunsett Mill on the river Ant (far right) are known far beyond Norfolk as images on jigsaw puzzles.

The river Thurne (above) rises near Martham Broad and joins the river Bure near St Benet's Abbey. The reedbeds in this area are an important habitat for birds; some such as the common crane quite rare. At How Hill Nature Reserve the reeds are harvested every year for roofing thatch.

## WORTH A VISIT

NORWICH

BLICKLING HALL

STRUMPSHAW FEN
NATURE RESERVE

TITCHWELL MARSH
NATURE RESERVE

HORSEY WINDPUMP

BURE VALLEY STEAM
RAILWAY

# STRATFORD-UPON-AVON

## *Warwickshire*

It is hard to ignore the presence of the Great Bard in Stratford. This was after all the birthplace of William Shakespeare (1564-1616), and today it is the home of the Royal Shakespeare Company. The river Avon flows through the town, past the Royal Shakespeare Theatre (right). In front of the theatre are the Bancroft Gardens where a statue of Shakespeare sits with four key figures from his plays: Prince Hal, Falstaff, Lady Macbeth and Hamlet (below, right). The collected bronze figures make up the Gower Memorial.

This house on Henley Street (right) is thought to be where Shakespeare was born and spent his childhood. A mile west of Stratford is the village of Shottery and Anne Hathaway's cottage (below) where Shakespeare courted his wife-to-be. A popular tourist destination, this substantial house is timbered, with a low thatched roof and lattice windows, and preserved as a prosperous Elizabethan family home.

### WORTH A VISIT

MARY ARDEN'S HOUSE

CHARLECOTE PARK AND
KINWARTON DOVECOTE

HIDCOTE MANOR
GARDEN

THE FLEECE INN,
BRETFERTON

KIFTSGATE COURT
GARDENS

COUGHTON COURT

UPTON HOUSE

# WARWICK CASTLE

## *Warwickshire*

WORTH A
VISIT

BADDESLEY
CLINTON

PACKWOOD HOUSE,
LAPWORTH

KENILWORTH
CASTLE

HERITAGE MOTOR
CENTRE

STRATFORD-UPON-
AVON

In 1752 Canaletto painted Warwick Castle, serene atop its hillside. It remains arguably the best preserved castle in Britain today.

Inside the castle walls, however, its turbulent history becomes clear. This was a castle built to withstand siege and attack. The towers were key to its defence, jutting out above the castle walls to give archers a clear line of sight sideways and downwards. On the land side stands Guy's Tower (1395), 12-sided and five storeys high. Shaped like a clover-leaf, Caesar's Tower (above) seems to grow out of the rocks above the river Avon. Concealed below is a grim dungeon and its *oubliette*, a dank hole in which prisoners were left to rot.

Today's visitors see how nobles, their servants and prisoners lived, and can even watch medieval jousting. Exhibitions document Warwick from its Norman beginnings to the Wars of the Roses (1453-85) and the English Civil War two centuries later.

The castle gardens are extensive and include river and island walks, a conservatory and a Victorian rose garden.

Top: water wheel in the mill and engine house with
Caesar's Tower in the background; above: children enjoy
viewing the armour in the Great Hall

# IRONBRIDGE

## *Shropshire*

WORTH A
VISIT

BUILDWAS ABBEY

BENTHALL HALL,
BROSELEY

THE WREKIN

BOSCOBEL HOUSE
AND THE ROYAL OAK

SEVERN VALLEY
RAILWAY

This quiet gorge was the birthplace of the Industrial Revolution. The ground-breaking decision to build a cast-iron bridge across the Severn at Coalbrookdale sprang from Abraham Darby's novel technique of smelting iron with coke rather than charcoal. Suddenly, high-quality iron could be made in vast quantities, affordably and at speed.

When the single-span bridge (left) opened in 1781, people came from far and wide to marvel at the structure. The town was so proud that it changed its name to Ironbridge.

The toll-house (above) still stands on the bridge, although today you must cross on foot. It now houses the Ironbridge Tourist Information Centre and one of the area's 10 museums, all celebrating aspects of the area's industrial past.

The butcher's shop at the Blists Hill open air museum (right) is one of several buildings showing what life would have been like in Shropshire during the Industrial Revolution.

# LIVERPOOL

*Merseyside*

### WORTH A VISIT

ALBERT DOCK

SPEKE HALL

NESS BOTANIC GARDENS

ANDERTON BOAT LIFT

CHESTER

AINTREE RACECOURSE

In the 1960s Liverpool's reputation soared as the home of the legendary Beatles, Gerry and the Pacemakers and many other bands. The Beatles first made their name at the Cavern Club in Mathew Street (above, centre). But the city has much to offer beyond the pop scene – two football clubs, the Toffeemen (Everton) and the Reds (Liverpool), its own Philharmonic Orchestra, and the Tate in the North gallery. The city's two cathedrals (far right) reflect its strong Protestant and Catholic traditions.

The city's best-known building is the Liver Building (above and near right), on Pier Head at the mouth of the River Mersey. Its bronze cormorants, the Liver Birds, spread their wings on two towers with the largest clockfaces in Britain. Liverpool has long been Britain's key port for sea trade with North America, from the days of cotton and slave-trading in the 18th century to the busy container port of today.

# MANCHESTER

*Lancashire*

A bout 100 miles from London, this dynamic cultural and commercial centre is the capital of the North-West and vies with Birmingham for the title of England's second city. The Roman name for Manchester, *Mancunium*, lives on today in the name given to the locals – Mancunians.

Neighbouring Salford has now merged into Manchester. Famous as the setting for *Coronation Street*, Salford's resurgence in recent years owes much to its illustrious son, LS Lowry. His paintings of "matchstick" working folk are housed in the ultra-modern Lowry Centre (left) in Salford Quays. The architect Daniel Libeskind designed the footbridge and the equally stunning Imperial War Museum North on the opposite bank of the Manchester Ship Canal.

In the centre of Manchester, more traditional buildings predominate. The 19th-century Gothic Town Hall and its imposing clock tower (right) loom over Albert Square. Nearby on St Peter's Square the classical lines of the much-loved Central Library (above right), date from 1934.

### WORTH A VISIT

HEATON HALL

WYTHENSHAWE HALL

DUNHAM MASSEY

LYME PARK

QUARRY BANK MILL AND STYAL ESTATE

TATTON PARK

# PEAK DISTRICT

*The southern Pennines, mostly in Derbyshire*

WORTH A VISIT

HARDWICK HALL

HADDON HALL

CALKE ABBEY

KEDLESTON

BLUE JOHN CAVERN

ILAM PARK

Drystone walls, gentle wooded or heather-covered slopes and stark rocky outcrops – and above it all, acres of sky. Add in some beautiful stately homes, a fascinating industrial heritage trail and the country's most popular theme park, Alton Towers, in Staffordshire, and you have the Peak District.

Eight miles north of Matlock stands Chatsworth House (above and right), the seat of the Duke of Devonshire. This graceful building combines classical architecture with a remarkable natural setting. The dramatic single plume of the Emperor Fountain is gravity-fed. In an age when we expect instant garden makeovers in a weekend, it is uplifting to see the fulfilment of the vision of Capability Brown, the master landscape designer, 250 years after he set about redesigning the grounds at Chatsworth.

What better contrast than to set out along Burbage Valley with its fast-flowing brook, up to Burbage Rocks (right). All this just eight miles from the heart of Sheffield. To the east lies the plateau of Burbage Moor. The Peak District also has a wealth of pretty villages, such as Castleton, together with the spa town of Buxton and the market town of Bakewell.

# BLACKPOOL

## *Lancashire*

Whence cheap air travel brought mass tourism to the Mediterranean during the 1960s, it eroded Blackpool's position as the favourite holiday destination for the North's factory workers. Nevertheless, this town with its three piers still offers more hotel beds than Portugal. About seven million people come every year to enjoy the thrills and spills of the giant rollercoasters and fairground rides of the Pleasure Beach all year round.

The famous Blackpool Illuminations light up five miles of the seafront every year from September to November. Blackpool Tower (above left) was designed in 1894 as a replica of the Eiffel Tower. People flock to take in the shows and go dancing in the ornate ballroom beneath the tower.

Meanwhile when the tide is out you can have a donkey ride on the sandy beach. The animals have a day off on Fridays, and after a busy summer they have their own holiday away from it all in green fields.

# YORK

*Yorkshire*

Y ork was an important city long before
London. Standing where the Foss and the
Ouse rivers meet, this was the capital of Roman
Britain for some 400 years. In the 9th century
the Vikings settled here, naming the town
Jorvik.

The Domesday Book described Jorvik 900
years ago as England's second largest city. The
Shambles (above), probably the best known
street in the whole of York today, was also listed
in that meticulous record of the Normans' new
kingdom. By 1872 there were 26 butchers on this

street alone – now there are none, but just like Guy Fawkes's birthplace, High Petergate (far left), its half-timbered medieval houses are more likely to be boutiques or restaurants.

The city is still dominated by its Gothic cathedral, York Minster (above). In July 1984 it lost its ancient oak roof and some of the stonework in a dramatic fire. Traditional craftsmen have restored the building to its former glory. Clifford's Tower (left) has a gory past: 150 Jews were massacred here in 1190 and Roger de Clifford hanged for treason in 1322.

## WORTH A VISIT

NATIONAL RAILWAY MUSEUM

YORK CASTLE

CASTLE HOWARD

BENINGBROUGH HALL

NEWBY HALL

YORKSHIRE AIR MUSEUM

## WORTH A VISIT

### BOLTON ABBEY

### PENNINE WAY

### CROOK GILL PACKHORSE BRIDGE

### STAINFORTH

### SETTLE-CARLISLE RAILWAY AND RIBBLEHEAD VIADUCT

### FOUNTAINS ABBEY

# YORKSHIRE DALES

*Yorkshire*

Most of Yorkshire's dales are named after their principal river. Hence Swaledale (left) follows the winding river Swale as it runs east from the village of Keld to the market town of Richmond. In the 18th century Swaledale was an important leadmining area, but today it is best known for its sheep and cheese, and of course the dramatic landscape.

The Vikings' name for a steep-sided valley, *dael*, is just one of the many echoes of this region's past. Some of the dales are wide and lush, others steep and narrow: all follow the course of their rivers as they head eastwards to the sea. The weathered limestone pavement at Malham (far left) shows all the classic signs of weathering, with deep cracks and crevices giving the impression of an intricate mosaic. This limestone scenery is typical of much of the Dales, particularly in the south.

Parallel to Swaledale runs Wensley-dale, where you will find Hardraw Force (above) in a tree-lined ravine. Britain's highest unbroken waterfall above ground, it drops 100ft (30m).

# LAKE DISTRICT

## *Cumbria*

This is not only a region of lakes but also where you find the highest points in England including Scafell and Helvellyn. The result is a spectacular variety of scenery in a relatively small area. Visitors often compare the serene beauty of Ullswater (left) with Lake Lucerne in Switzerland. Old steamers ply the three reaches of the lake as it zigzags for seven miles (12km) through the surrounding hills.

While Ullswater is the longest of the lakes, the relatively shallow Derwent Water (below left) just south of Keswick is the widest at 1.25 miles. Derwent Water has seven islands – and sometimes another "floating island" surfaces, pushed up by marsh gases. A favourite viewpoint is the old packhorse bridge known as Ashness Bridge (below), looking north across Derwent Water to the peaks of Skiddaw.

Those who prefer more rugged landscapes will appreciate Wast Water (right) further west, with dramatic scree slopes sweeping down to its eastern shore.

### WORTH A VISIT

HOLKER HALL

RYDAL MOUNT

HILL TOP

MIRE HOUSE

RAVENGLASS AND
ESKDALE RAILWAY

TOWNEND

THE BOWDER STONE

# DURHAM

## *County Durham*

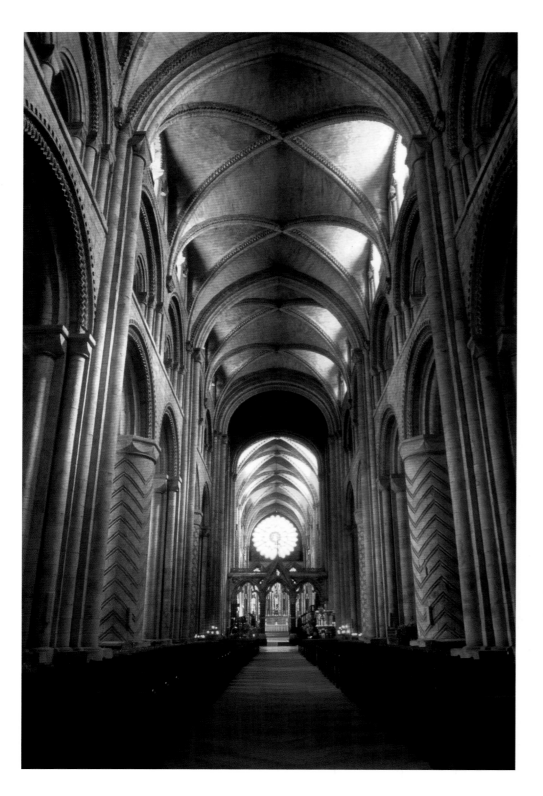

Ounty Durham stretches from the North Sea in the east to the Pennine hills in the west. Much of the county town, Durham, is tucked into a peninsula formed by the river Wear.

England's first historian, the Venerable Bede, lies buried in the magnificent cathedral, which can trace its history back 1,000 years to a group of monks from Lindisfarne. Under the Normans, Benedictine monks built the cathedral and the nearby Durham Castle. St Cuthbert's shrine ensured that a steady flow of pilgrims kept the cathedral's coffers full and a busy market town grew up around the cathedral.

In 1832 the castle became the home of England's third university, University College, Durham. Today Durham Castle, the Cathedral and the landlocked island on which they are sited is a World Heritage site. The author Bill Bryson considers Durham "the best cathedral on Planet Earth". Its soaring nave (left) has been an inspiration to many, and the bell tower houses a magnificent ring of 10 bells.

### WORTH A VISIT

| | |
|---|---|
| AUCKLAND CASTLE, BISHOP AUCKLAND | BEAMISH NORTH OF ENGLAND OPEN AIR MUSEUM |
| BARNARD CASTLE | |
| | WALDRIDGE FELL |
| CROOK HALL | |
| | OTTER TRUST, BOWES |
| RABY CASTLE | |

# NEWCASTLE AND GATESHEAD

*Tyne and Wear*

Antony Gormley's iconic sculpture, the Angel of the North (far right, top) spreads its wings on a hill just outside Gateshead. The public perception of the twin cities of Newcastle and Gateshead, either side of the Tyne, has changed dramatically in the last decade. Now the secret is out: this is a vibrant place, with an important history and stylish contemporary architecture.

Newcastle has a long tradition of radical bridge design. The Tyne Bridge (above), a compression arch suspended-deck bridge, opened in 1928. Beyond is the 19th-century Armstrong Swing Bridge which pivots on a central pier in the river, and beyond that the High Level Bridge.

The most recent addition opened in 2002. The Gateshead Millennium Bridge (right) is an almost ethereal structure that can be "tilted like the opening of an eye" to allow ships to pass upriver.

Classical buildings have their place here

too – only Bath and London can boast more listed Georgian buildings than the city centre of Newcastle. The elegant glass-roofed Central Arcade (1906) on Grey Street is a world away from the modern Eldon Square shopping complex just round the corner.

## WORTH A VISIT

BALTIC CENTRE FOR CONTEMPORARY ART

BLACKFRIARS

TOWN WALLS

TYNEMOUTH PRIORY

BEDE'S WORLD

# HADRIAN'S WALL

*Northumbria*

Historians believe the Emperor Hadrian may have modelled his wall to protect the northern frontier of Roman Britain on the Great Wall of China. Hadrian's Wall stretches 73 miles (117km) across from the Solway Firth to the river Tyne and took six years to build, from AD122-128. The Barbarian hordes on the other side would have faced a 15ft-high (4m) stone wall surmounted by another six feet (2m) of timber. Sixteen forts, another 80 mile-castles and many signal turrets ensured speedy communication and reinforcement along the line.

Excavations at Vindolanda Fort (near right) just south of the wall have shown that there was a significant civilian settlement that grew up around the Roman fort, with workshops, temples, a travellers' lodge and bathhouse. The view (far right) is the landscape east of Housesteads Fort. At Crag Lough (above) Hadrian's Wall follows the line of the rocky outcrop, part of Whin Sill. The smooth dolerite rocks of the crag here are a popular challenge for rock-climbers.

WORTH A
VISIT

CHESTERS FORT

HOUSESTEADS
FORT

GEORGE
STEPHENSON'S
BIRTHPLACE,
WYLAM

WALLINGTON

PENNINE WAY

# LINDISFARNE AND BAMBURGH

*Nine miles south-east of Berwick-on-Tweed*

Lindisfarne is known locally as Holy Island. St Aidan (near right) founded a monastery here in AD634, a centre of early Christianity. Later that century Bishop Eadfrith and his monks illuminated the incomparable Lindisfarne Gospels in honour of his predecessor St Cuthbert.

A century after the Vikings burnt down the monastery in AD793 the monks left the island, taking St Cuthbert's relics and the Lindisfarne Gospels with them. Today Durham Cathedral and the British Museum are custodians of Cuthbert's remains and the Lindisfarne Gospels respectively.

The island is now home to 150 people. Its 16th-century castle (above) and the ruins of the Priory (far right), dissolved by Henry VIII in 1536, are popular with visitors. At low water you can follow the line of stakes from the island along Pilgrims' Way, a causeway to the village of Beale on the mainland. At the far end of the bay, on a basalt crag overlooking the sandy beach, stands Bamburgh Castle (above right) where Robert the Bruce was once imprisoned.

# CARDIFF

## *South Glamorgan*

Remarkably green and uncrowded, Cardiff is Europe's youngest capital city. It sits at the mouth of the Taff, Rhymney and Ely rivers and at its heart stands Cardiff Castle, complete with clock tower (above). The living quarters of the castle were given a Gothic makeover in the 1860s.

In the 20th century Cardiff was transformed. City Hall (far right) opened when it achieved city status in 1905. Fifty years later Cardiff was proclaimed the capital of the principality, and in 1999 it became home to the Welsh Assembly.

Ultra-modern buildings symbolise the vigour of the city today. The Cardiff Bay Visitor Centre, down by the old coal docks, is known as "the Tube" because of its striking design. In 2004, the Wales Millennium Centre (far right) was opened as an exciting new venue for classical music, opera and concerts. Best known of all is the gleaming Millennium Stadium (right) with its retractable roof, which firmly places Cardiff in the international arena for rugby, football and speedway.

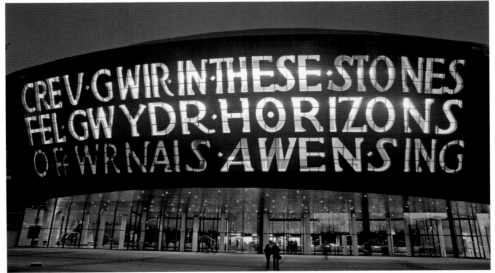

## WORTH A VISIT

WELSH ASSEMBLY
BUILDING

TREDEGAR HOUSE

CASTELL COCH

RHONDDA HERITAGE
PARK

PARK CEFN ONN

COSMESTON LAKES
AND PARK

OFFA'S DYKE PATH

# GOWER PENINSULA

*West of Swansea*

When you see the magnificent coastline, it is not surprising to learn that the Gower peninsula is the most visited part of Wales after Snowdonia. It is just 16 miles (26km) by seven miles (11km) wide and justifiably classed as an area of outstanding natural beauty.

On the southern tip of Swansea Bay lies the village of Mumbles, with its lighthouse (right) and the renowned cluster of pubs where the poet Dylan Thomas used to drink. Further along the southern coast is Three Cliffs Bay (above), popular with rock climbers who tackle the 65ft (20m) limestone cliffs that stretch out into the sea.

In the far south-west of the peninsula the village of Rhossili perches on cliffs. From here you can see for miles over the bay to Lundy Island and enjoy glorious sunsets over the sea. Below the cliffs the powerful waves of the Atlantic Ocean draw surfers to the three-mile long beach. At low tide you can walk out to the rocky outcrop known as Worm's Head (left).

## WORTH A VISIT

ARTHUR'S STONE

OYSTERMOUTH CASTLE

OXWICH BAY

PORT EYNON POINT AND CLIFFTOP PATH

BOAT TRIP TO LUNDY ISLAND

ST ILLTYD CHURCH

# ST DAVID'S

*West Pembrokeshire*

With a population of just 2,000 Britain's smallest city feels more like a village. St David's takes its name from the patron saint of Wales who was born nearby in the 6th century and established a monastery on this spot.

In the Middle Ages Edward the Confessor was one of the many pilgrims who made their way to the 12th-century cathedral (right) to pray at the shrine of St David. Today tourists come to admire the medieval wood and stonework and many tombs that have survived the centuries. In contrast, the once-lavish Bishop's Palace with its impressive central courtyard and many-arched parapets stands next to the cathedral (above right). It fell victim to the Reformation and now lies in ruins.

St David's is surrounded by the Pembrokeshire Coast National Park, and the coastal path runs along the peninsula. The rugged coastline teems with wildlife, and from April to July the 400ft (120m) cliffs on nearby Ramsey Island (above, on the horizon) house important breeding colonies of choughs and wheatears. In the autumn grey seals breed here too.

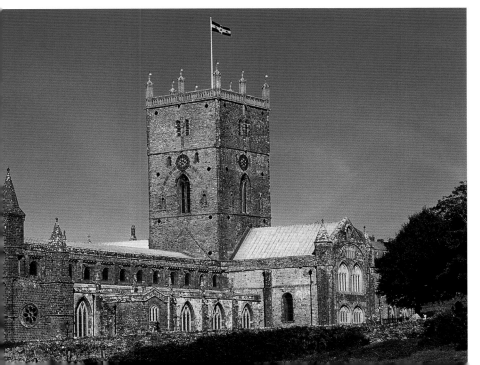

# HARLECH

*Six miles south of Porthmadog, Gwynedd*

WORTH A
VISIT

SNOWDONIA
NATIONAL PARK

COED Y BRENIN
FOREST PARK

RHAEADR
MAWDDACH AND
PISTYLL Y CAIN
WATERFALLS,
AND THE OLD
GWYNFYNYDD
GOLDMINE

LLANFAIR SLATE
CAVERNS

PORTMEIRION
VILLAGE

Incredibly it took just seven years to build the stronghold of Harlech Castle, part of the iron ring of castles Edward I built to subdue the Welsh. The waters of Tremadoc Bay used to lap the rocks at the foot of the castle, but are now half a mile away.

Harlech has a long history of siege: if the rocks on its three land sides failed to hold back the attackers, then the concentric series of outer and inner walls and the twin-towered gatehouse kept them at bay. Meanwhile supplies could be smuggled in by sea. In 1294 the Welsh rebel Madog failed, but in 1404

Owain Glyndwr triumphed by securing the sea approaches, only to lose it in turn to the English five years later.

During the Wars of the Roses a particularly grim siege culminated in 1468 with a Yorkist victory over Dafydd ap Ieuan. The song *Men of Harlech* commemorates his struggle. During the Civil War (1642-48) Harlech was the last Royalist stronghold to fall.

The statue of the mythical giant king of Britain, Bendigeidfran, and his nephew Gwern (right) stands near the gatehouse, a comment on the futility of war.

# SNOWDONIA

*Gwynedd*

Snowdonia National Park is the backdrop for much of central and north-west Wales. Its best-known mountain is the five-peaked Yr Wyddfa, otherwise known as Snowdon (right), seen here with the waters of Llyn Llydaw in the foreground. At 3,560ft (1,085m), Snowdon is Wales's highest mountain. It is star-shaped with six ridges, each fanning out into a cwm (valley) with its own distinct character.

To the south of Snowdonia the looming slopes of Cadair Idris dominate the landscape. The highest of its three peaks is known as Pen y Gadair: below it the "pewter bowl" of Llyn y Gadair (above) glistens at the foot of a steep bank of scree on the mountain's north-western flank. Visitors and residents alike treasure the view of Cadair Idris from the north across the Mawddach Estuary.

Below Cadair Idris are the Cregennen Lakes (above right). The craggy face of Tyrrau Mawr looms above the waters and at several points close to the lakes there are magnificent views of the Mawddach Estuary, Barmouth and the distant Lleyn Peninsula.

## WORTH A VISIT

TALYLLYN RAILWAY AND
DOLGOCH FALLS

CASTELL Y BERE

CENTRE FOR ALTERNATIVE
TECHNOLOGY,
MACHYNLLETH

COED-Y-BRENIN AND
SNOWDONIA FOREST PARKS

PENRHYN CASTLE

# PORTMEIRION

*Just south of Porthmadog, Gwynedd*

One man's vision became reality when the architect Clough Williams-Ellis created the village of Portmeirion. When he bought this small peninsula the hotel (below left) already existed, but overambitious landscaping projects had bankrupted all the previous owners.

The project dominated Clough's life from 1925-1976, and the village that you see today is very much as he planned it. It is more Mediterranean than Welsh, with houses painted in whites and pastels and palm trees swaying in the breeze. Some people consider it simply quirky, but Clough's designs incorporate architectural objects salvaged elsewhere into a harmonious whole.

Two freestanding columns in the Piazza (above) are topped with statues of Burmese dancers. The Gloriette with its four 18th-century columns is simply a façade with trompe l'oeil windows. Behind is Telford's Tower, a homage to the engineer who built the Menai Bridge. Beautiful gardens with woodland walks extend to the tip of the peninsula.

Clough's dramatic opening gesture was to build the Campanile (above left) which drew on bell-towers he had seen in Italy. In 1961 when he was 80 years old, Clough put the finishing touches to his Pantheon dome, as ever living up to his motto: "Cherish the past, adorn the present, construct for the future."

# CAERNARFON

*South-eastern end of the Menai Strait, Gwynedd*

WORTH A
VISIT

SEGONTIUM
ROMAN FORT

PLAS NEWYDD

ANGLESEY SEA
ZOO

PARC
GLYNLLIFON

SNOWDONIA
NATIONAL PARK

As with the other castles in the iron ring built by the English King Edward I, Caernarfon Castle (right) was not raised to protect the Welsh but to impose English rule upon them. This is certainly an awe-inspiring fortress, with its octagonal towers and crenellated walls (nine feet thick in some places) but it was not impregnable. In 1294 it was briefly taken by Welsh nationalists, and Cromwell's troops seized it in 1646. Edward I dedicated his infant son here in 1284 as the Prince of Wales; the traditional title passed to the monarch's eldest son but six centuries went by before the next investiture was held at Caernarfon.

The castle is very much at the heart of the town (above), which sits at the mouth of the Seiont, overlooking the southern end of the Menai Strait. The harbour bustles with fishing boats and pleasure craft. Take a walk through the narrow streets of the old town and you will probably hear Welsh spoken as a matter of course.

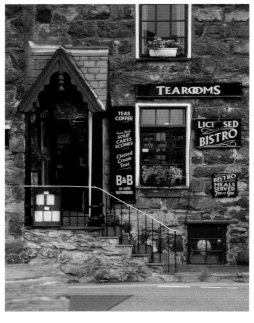

# MENAI STRAIT

*Between Gwynedd and Anglesey*

The engineer Thomas Telford's designs, at the start of the 19th century, for the improvement of the important London to Holyhead route for travellers to Ireland included a controversial suspension bridge (left) across the Menai Strait. The Menai Bridge you see today is still Telford's design, albeit much modified since it opened in 1824.

Beaumaris Castle (above) at the northern end of the strait was the last of Edward I's great series of fortresses, designed to strengthen his hold on Wales. Though never finished, it is considered by many to be the most technically perfect. Inside the seawater moat is an intriguing symmetrical layout, "a box within a box" with cleverly angled walls and staggered entrances that would have allowed defenders precious extra time to see off their attackers.

In Llanfairpwll the elegant Plas Newydd, the home of the Marquess of Anglesey, offers wonderful views across the strait to Snowdonia. It is best known for the vast panoramic mural (right) in the dining room painted by Rex Whistler.

# CONWY

## *The north-eastern end of the Menai Strait*

Travel north along the Welsh coastline from the Menai Strait and you come to Conwy Bay, dominated by the battlements of Conwy Castle (above right). One of Edward I's earliest Welsh castles, it perches on cliffs above the town. You can still walk along much of the old walls that enclosed the old whole town.

Two years after he designed the Menai Bridge, Thomas Telford turned his hand to the much smaller Conwy Suspension Bridge (below) across the river Conwy. Its graceful lines flow from supporting towers that echo the shape of the castle's turrets. Close by is a tubular rail bridge designed by Robert Stephenson.

Despite a turbulent past, the walled town of Conwy (far right, below) holds some medieval gems. The half-timbered Aberconwy House belonged to a merchant in the 14th century, and Plas Mawr, which dates from 1585, is a beautifully preserved lime-rendered Elizabethan townhouse.

Walk along Quayside and you will find Britain's smallest house. This tiny red house stands next to the river that flows close to the castle. Its two storeys combined are just over 10ft high and it was once home to a six-foot fisherman. Not surprisingly it is no longer inhabited, but you can pay to take a peek inside.

## WORTH A VISIT

BODNANT GARDEN

PENRHYN CASTLE

TREFRIW WOOLLEN MILLS AND SPA

ABER FALLS, ABERGWYNGREGYN

SNOWDONIA NATIONAL PARK

# EDINBURGH

*Scotland's capital city*

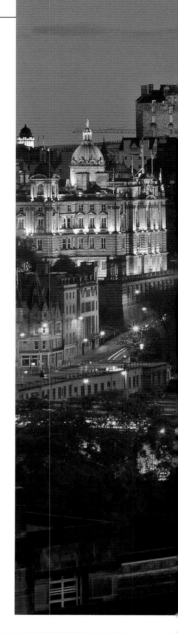

Edinburgh's Princes Street (below) has something for everyone – fashionable shops; the Princes Street Gardens along the south side, complete with a funfair and ice rink at Christmas; the monument (right of picture) to Scotland's favourite author Sir Walter Scott and his dog. It runs parallel to the famous Royal Mile, which has linked the palace of Holyrood House with Edinburgh Castle since the Middle Ages. Many of Edinburgh's key attractions lie along these two thoroughfares.

From the city's much-loved Calton Hill the panorama sweeps across the Old Town to Edinburgh Castle (right). Night and day the Castle, perched on its volcanic crag, dominates the city. In August the castle esplanade is packed with 217,000 spectators for the annual Edinburgh Military Tattoo (below, far right): massed pipes and drums vie with military marching bands and Highland dancers, and in the closing moments a lone piper plays a lament on the castle ramparts.

## WORTH A VISIT

SCOTTISH PARLIAMENT BUILDING,
HOLYROOD

ROYAL BOTANIC GARDEN

ST GILES CATHEDRAL

NATIONAL GALLERY OF SCOTLAND AND
NATIONAL GALLERY OF MODERN ART

CALTON HILL PANTHEON

HOLYROOD HOUSE

HOPETOUN HOUSE

ROSSLYN CHAPEL

# FORTH BRIDGES

*Firth of Forth*

In Alfred Hitchcock's thriller *The 39 Steps* the hero escaped from a train on the Forth Railway Bridge (left) to dangle 150ft (45m) above the chilly waters of the Firth of Forth. In 1890 this dramatic structure was the world's first major steel bridge. It still carries over 180 trains a day along the east coast to and from Edinburgh.

Such a huge structure – the central span is over 1,100 yards (1km) long – has inevitably required continuous maintenance, and "painting the Forth Bridge" became a metaphor for an endless (and unrewarding) task. But new technology now means it will only need to be repainted every 30 years.

Seen from South Queensferry, the graceful suspension road bridge (below left) that opened in 1964 complements the solid cantilever rail bridge. Along the coast, the tiny Lady's Tower at Elie Ness (below) stands alone looking south. In the 1750s a local aristocrat sent out a servant to ring a bell when she was bathing in the sea warning all the villagers to stay away.

# GLASGOW

## *Greater Glasgow and Clyde Valley*

In recent years Glasgow has become a major player on the culture trail and is now a vibrant international centre. In the last two decades the city has cleaned, preened and planted, rundown buildings have been transformed into energetic new businesses and its considerable cultural assets, new and old, have been brought into focus as never before. Since 1990 when Glasgow was the European City of Culture there has been no holding back.

Kelvingrove Art Gallery and Museum (right) is the Glaswegians' favourite Edwardian building, and the most visited museum in the UK outside London. The building itself is in a Spanish Baroque style, and its wide-ranging collections include major Impressionist paintings.

At the heart of the city is George Square (below right) with statues of Scotland's greats including Robert Burns, James Watt and Sir Walter Scott. The river Clyde (below) was key to Glasgow's commercial prominence as a port and textile centre in the 18th and 19th centuries. Today the Science Centre and the Scottish Exhibition Centre grace the riverbanks.

## WORTH A VISIT

# Loch Lomond

*Stirling*

Twenty miles north-west of Glasgow, across the Kilpatrick Hills, lies Scotland's most famous loch. The tranquil, cold waters of Loch Lomond run 600ft (196m) deep in places. This is Britain's largest freshwater loch, 24 miles long and five miles wide (38km by 8km).

Most visitors will hope to catch the classic view of the loch's mirror-like waters reflecting the snow-capped peak of Ben Lomond (left), from the pier in the village of Luss. Although the mountain qualifies as a Munro (a peak over 3,000ft/914m), serious climbers are disdainful of the easy trek to the summit. On a clear day, however, the views over the loch and Southern Highlands are enough to raise the spirits of the most hardened cynic.

The loch is widest at its southern end, where the paddle-steamer *Maid of the Loch* (above) is permanently moored at Balloch. You can hire a Drascombe lugger (below) for the day to sail along the coast and to the many islands.

## WORTH A VISIT

BUCINCH AND CEARDACH

CRARAE GARDEN

THE HILL HOUSE,
HELENSBURGH

GEILSTON GARDEN

WEST HIGHLAND WAY

REST AND BE THANKFUL

# ST ANDREWS

*Fife*

The centre of St Andrews still shows its medieval origins, when it was Scotland's religious and intellectual hub. St Andrews University is the third oldest in Britain, dating from 1410, and it is widely considered to be one of Scotland's best. Its School of Divinity is housed in the original 16th-century buildings of St Mary's College (below, far right).

For a panoramic view of St Andrews Cathedral (above) and the town beyond you can climb St Rule's Tower. The vast cathedral was consecrated in 1390, when Robert the Bruce is said to have ridden up the aisle on a horse. In 1559 the Reformist John Knox, founder of the Church of Scotland, so stirred up a mob with his fiery oratory against "popery" that they tore down the cathedral, leaving the ruins you see today.

Golfers everywhere consider St Andrews as the home of golf. For more than 250 years the Royal and Ancient Golf Club (right) has been the arbiter of the rules of the sport. On the 18th fairway of the Old Course, golfers cross the Old Swilken Bridge as they near the clubhouse.

## WORTH A VISIT

St Andrews Botanic Gardens

Eden Estuary nature reserve

Hill of Tarvit

Scottish Fisheries Museum

Kellie Castle and garden

Falkland Palace, garden and
Old Burgh

# GLEN COE

## Highlands

### WORTH A VISIT

BEN NEVIS

BEN LAWERS NATIONAL NATURE RESERVE

GLENFINNAN MONUMENT

INVERLOCHY CASTLE

If you are walking the challenging West Highland Way, you come to the wilds of Rannoch Moor (above) with its rocks, lochs and mountains – here you see Ba Loch with Black Mount in the background. Where Glen Etive meets the pass of Glen Coe, Stob Dearg (right) rises at the end of the Buachaille Etive Mor ridge. This peak is a favourite with walkers and climbers of all abilities.

Many people still feel a frisson as they enter Glen Coe, an echo of the horrific massacre of the Clan MacDonald in January 1692. The MacDonalds had given their traditional rivals, the Campbells, shelter for 10 days before their guests turned on them on the order of King William III. Many of those who escaped died of hunger and exposure in the surrounding hills.

Today Glen Coe is promoted as "the cradle of Scottish mountaineering". The history of the glen and the surrounding area is recorded at the eco-friendly Glencoe Visitor Centre (left) at the western end of the glen. The centre, which is run by the Scottish National Trust, opened in 2002; it contains a fascinating "Living on the Edge" exhibition featuring the area's ecology, heritage and climbing history.

# LOCH NESS

*Between Inverness and Fort Augustus*

You will probably not spot the legendary monster in the beautiful waters of Loch Ness that stretch from Inverness to Fort Augustus, but you are certain to see a rich variety of birds – if you are lucky you may even see an osprey fishing for salmon or brown trout.

The view down the loch (above) from Dores village on the south bank gives an idea of its sweeping grandeur. Six major rivers flow into this deep, long loch, and the short river Ness in turn drains the water into the sea at Inverness.

By Drumnadrochit on the north bank, the ruins of Castle Urquhart sit on Strone Point (above right). This used to be the largest of all Scotland's castles: it was much enlarged by the English King Edward I. In his continuing efforts to subdue the country he became known as the Hammer of the Scots.

At the southern end of the loch lies Fort Augustus. Boats must pass through the lock (right) to enter the Caledonian Canal, which continues to Fort William via the spectacular Neptune's Staircase locks.

## WORTH A
VISIT

MONIACK CASTLE
AND WINERY

LOCH NESS
MONSTER VISITOR
CENTRE,
DRUMNADROCHIT

LOCH RUTHVEN
NATURE RESERVE

COILTIE GARDENS
AND DIVACH FALLS

ABRIACHAN
GARDENS

# INVERNESS AND CULLODEN

## *Highlands*

Greig Street footbridge (above) is one of several bridges that span the river Ness and Caledonian Canal in Inverness as they approach the Moray Firth. Thomas Telford built the canal to link the North Sea and the Irish Sea.

Inverness is often called the crossroads of the Highlands. The surrounding region has the lowest population density in Europe, but this is one of Europe's fastest growing cities. Its castle (above right), on the banks of the River Ness, was built in the 1830s, not to subdue the town but to run it and to house the law courts.

For a thought-provoking piece of Highland history come to Culloden Moor (below, far right), the site of the last land battle fought in Britain. You can walk round the battlefield where the hopes of Bonnie Prince Charlie, the pretender to the British throne, and his Jacobite army were savagely shattered in 1746 by the Duke of Cumberland's army. The bloody battle lasted just an hour but the story of the prince's escape to France was told for generations. Some of his wounded followers were less fortunate: they took refuge in a barn at Old Leanach farm (right) only to be killed by Cumberland's men.

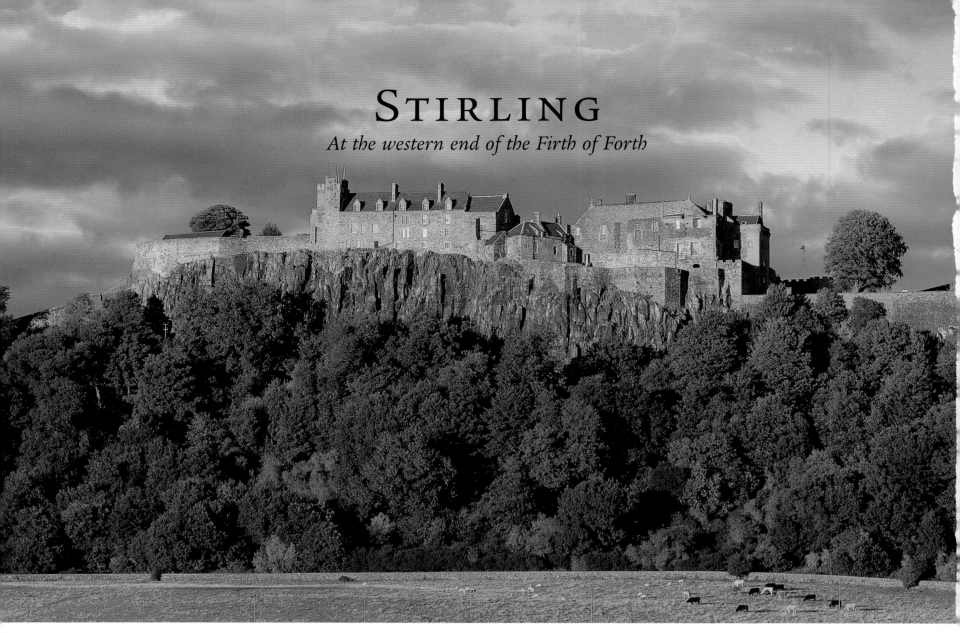

# STIRLING

*At the western end of the Firth of Forth*

The childhood home of Mary Queen of Scots, Stirling is the grandest castle in Scotland. It looms over the scene of some of the nation's most important battles and the castle was frequently besieged as England fought to dominate the Scottish kingdom. In 1297 William Wallace triumphed over Edward I's army at Stirling Bridge. Seventeen years later the English were once again defeated by Robert the Bruce at Bannockburn.

William Wallace and his pivotal role in Scotland's struggle for independence are remembered at the nearby Wallace Monument, which overlooks the river Forth. Though he never won another battle for Scotland, his execution for treason in 1305 succeeded in stoking the Scots' determination to achieve independence. Robert the Bruce was crowned king at Scone the following year.

Mary Queen of Scots' life ended on the English scaffold but ironically her son, James, was to unite the two countries as the first Stuart king of England and Scotland in 1567.

WORTH A VISIT

STIRLING

ALLOA TOWER

BANNOCKBURN

CASTLE CAMPBELL AND DOLLAR GLEN

GARTMORN DAM